The Ways We Live

Michelle Jovin, M.A.

People live in lots of places.

People have ways to stay cozy.

It is cold where we live!

We can stay warm.

Our home helps us stay warm.

Our clothes help us stay warm too.

It is hot where we live!

We can stay cool.

Our home helps us stay cool.

Our clothes help us stay cool too.

It is rainy where we live!

We can stay dry.

Our home helps us
stay dry.

Our clothes help us stay dry too.

What is it like where you live?

How do you stay cozy?

Draw It!

What if you lived at the North Pole? What would your life be like?

1. Draw your home at the North Pole.

2. Draw your clothes.

3. Show how you will stay warm.

Consultant

Chrissy Johnson, M.Ed.
Elementary School Teacher
Cedar Point Elementary

Publishing Credits

Rachelle Cracchiolo, M.S.Ed., *Publisher*
Aubrie Nielsen, M.S.Ed., *EVP of Content Development*
Emily R. Smith, M.A.Ed., *VP of Content Development*
Véronique Bos, *Creative Director*
Robin Erickson, *Art Director*
Michelle Jovin, M.A., *Associate Editor*
Fabiola Sepulveda, *Graphic Designer*

Image Credits: p.19 Valeria Fabregas; all other images from iStock and/or Shutterstock.

TCM Teacher Created Materials
5482 Argosy Avenue
Huntington Beach, CA 92649
www.tcmpub.com
ISBN 978-1-0876-0383-4